ACTORS:
Becoming a Business

Copyright © 2018 by Emmett Ferguson

Edited by Kathleen Roy

Published by Emmett Ferguson

ISBN-13: 978-1721519477 | **ISBN-10:** 1721519475

*Inspired by the many actors
dedicating so much to their art and craft.*

Contents

Foreword

By Bob Telford

In my nearly 40 years in the entertainment business, I have seen many changes. There have been new technologies, more content platforms, evolving approaches to casting, representation, and production. But the one thing that has not changed is that this is a business. Many times, I have heard people say the phrase, "It's called show business, not show art!". That said, I think of myself as a professional in this industry.

I had the good fortune to have a reasonably good career as an actor and director. I have worked in the theater, commercials, TV, and film. I have always tried to stay abreast of the latest trends in all areas of this industry and most importantly, understanding my responsibility as a professional and I feel that has been a big factor in my having achieved that success.

I met Emmett when I cast him in a project which I was directing. We had a successful run, and I felt blessed to have him as a part of my cast. When we finished the show, I stayed in touch with him as I do with many of the talented people I work with. We had several meetings where he asked my advice on projects that he was developing. As I have always done throughout my career, I agreed to offer any support and information that would be helpful.

In one of our meetings, he mentioned that he was writing a book on the business side of the entertainment industry geared specifically towards actors. He asked if I would give it a read and offer my thoughts. I did not hesitate, and I said yes. I was thoroughly impressed by the depth and breadth of its contents.

I find it fascinating how many times actors will spend countless amounts of their hard-earned cash on all kinds of acting technique books and not give the business side any consideration. I can testify to the benefits I have received by making sure that I balanced my continued professional education with both the art and business acumen. I feel we as professionals need both to succeed.

I will warn you right now; there is a tremendous amount of information contained in this book. It may take several readings or repeated referrals to various chapters to grasp all that this book has to offer, but I think it is well worth the effort. I applauded Emmett on writing this book, and I encourage anyone pursuing a professional acting career to give it a read.

I would like to close this by quoting Andy Warhol. He said, "Making money is **art** and working is **art,** and good **business** is the best **art**." I think this best sums up my approach to this incredible industry. I hope you do the same.

Bob Telford

Introduction

Acting is a career for many who in the past, dropped everything and moved to areas like Hollywood and New York to pursue their dreams. Today, new opportunities are arising through the internet for people to launch their entertainment careers no matter where they are. At the same time, states such as Texas, Georgia, Louisiana, and more become attractive to actors as more productions happen outside of California. The opportunity to pursue this dream career is better than ever.

When opportunity becomes more abundant, so then does the talent pool. There is a beautiful thing about Hollywood specifically, and that is how focused the city is on one specific goal: creating the most visually entertaining movies, television shows, commercials, and more, in the world. And businesses from entertainment to IT hardware are taking part in it in some way (think product placements and new marketing tactics). Even those who are not specifically in the industry go through their daily lives and likely interact with at least one entertainment professional or actor per day.

As the technology giants of the world realize the tremendous demand for content to keep peoples' eyes on their mobile devices, platforms, and services, opportunities for actors increases. These new social changes create a huge sea of opportunity and challenges.

Today, to pursue the dream of becoming an actor, some will find luck very early in their careers. Some will only work occasionally while spending most of their time in what is called a "survival job." Some may not work at all finding that they are unprepared for the challenges and head back to their hometowns. And others will find ways to carve their paths opening themselves to their self-created luck which they will act on.

This book is for actors who have heard plenty of important advice on topics such as headshots, classes, agents, cities to move to, risk, auditioning, and more. The answers are found around the internet, in the classes you take, and in the coffee shops in Hollywood. This book ties all of these topics together into how they all fit into the bigger picture: business.

Before moving forward, it is important to realize this industry, like many others, is filled with frauds and risks, and all "business ideas" should be pursued with careful consideration. This book can help actors see the bigger picture for themselves to determine if something will truly bring value to them, or if it is a waste.

If an actor is seeking a long-term career, he or she can open up to new ways of thinking and approach to the industry. While developing the craft is a major aspect of success, many can become so dependent on the craft, that they forget that there is more at stake than simply their ability to say a sentence. Millions of dollars are often on the line. Jobs and reputations are often on the line. Brands and relationships are on the line.

This book aims to provide an actor or future actor with a way to view his or her career as a business. While this can seem like a huge complex topic, it is not. Actors who are actively pursuing work do many activities as a business, but simply do not have explicit definitions of what they are doing.

For example, teaming up with an agent or manager is about more than finding someone to connect you with the right people who can put you in their movies. Most likely, when you are a beginning film actor, you will sign with an agent or manager who is too busy to help actors much as he or she starts out. Finding an agent or manager is about building your business and growing a team of professionals around you to create a profitable business operation for you and them.

Sometimes it is up to the actor to start those tough conversations with an agent or manager. Sometimes it only takes a call, sometimes it requires a few stops by the office, and other times a relationship might not work, and you have to refresh. Because I had a lot of sales and marketing experience, I made a series of cold email campaigns to directors and producers which also introduced my agent.

With that said, there are differences when seeking clients if you are opening a restaurant business, or launching a mobile app company then you do when you are starting your business as an actor. There are even some fundamental ideas that can help you succeed. You will want to set up operations, research and development, financial education, marketing, sales, and a great product or service. Again, many actors already work on their business, and this book helps provide ways of defining their work that can help them grow.

Here is how all of it comes together. You might have searched online for something akin to "how to become an actor." Answers may include network, buy better headshots, post content, sign up for a website, build a resume when you have no experience, and the list goes on. These can all be very confusing without really knowing why they are important, especially in an industry environment where every person you talk to has an opposite opinion on a topic from the last. This does not mean there are no standards; it just means it is an artistic industry, and many things are subjective. Therefore, take note of what you learn from more established people. The lessons may not always apply to you, and you can test them out and see what works.

As you read this book, envision yourself as both the product/service and Chief Executive Officer of <Your Name Here> Entertainment Enterprises. Throughout this book, you may find answers you can apply now at this very moment to grow your business and better or different ways to approach your acting career. Because the business of acting is unique, while the overall structure may differ from other businesses, the fundamentals are still valid and critical to success.

1. Entrepreneur

We start off our journey with the statement that actors start as entrepreneurs even though they may not realize. Some eventually go on to become household names, others keep regular steady careers but choose not to take on stardom. Others find that they prefer to pursue different dreams similar to how some apps, brands, and restaurants become globally recognized, some stay mom and pop, and others are not recognized. The actor and entrepreneur are launching a new brand and business which may or may not succeed. That is the risk one chooses in any endeavor.

In choosing to become an entrepreneur, an actor becomes an adventurer and someone who sees a bigger picture for him or herself and the world. One who lives an incredibly interesting life to help make the real world more interesting. One who is adaptable and capable of overcoming tough challenges. And one who wants to create and be a part of some of the greatest stories ever told.

The actor chooses to go after their vision of success even with the risks involved. There is no settling for mediocre at this point. It is ambitious for actors to portray some of the greatest fictional (and non-fictional) figures in our world. The actor entrepreneur knows the tremendous value his or her likeness brings to the world and wants to get it out there. And the top actors have goals that are measurable. Consider the stories you hear about how many awards an actor has, and how more awards contribute to their credibility.

An entrepreneurs' success is in large part determined by his or her ability to focus on a specific purpose. Often this is done by creating great habits when dealing with people, work, and self which requires a fit mind and body that synergizes to create an exceptional likeness for the big screen. Maintaining physical and mental health as an actor through exercise, diet, and sleep habits can influence success. Just as memorization of a script and character development demands incredible focus, so does the bigger picture of an actors' goals.

Many actors use their brand to focus on topics such as global warming, education, health, and many more. When overcoming obstacles, it can become easier to maintain optimism by keeping your mind on the greater goal you wish to accomplish.

One of the biggest defining factors of entrepreneurs is that they take on calculated risk even when opposed by many. They realize there will always be naysayers in every endeavor, as well as the chance of failure. However, the risk is not blind. These entrepreneurs realize life passes too quickly to live without taking any risks. To create an acting career that survives the long term, try taking on greater challenges even if some may fail. These actors visualize the reward they want and make it specific.

Actors are great entrepreneurs because they are creative at heart. They view the world differently and sometimes take on jobs where they experience the world from someone else's eyes. They study their roles carefully, so they can discover what their life is like. The actor must dig deep and study the world around him or herself.

Entrepreneurs know there are ways to improve the world around them. There is a realization that things are more than just what is on the surface. The creative comes up with great and interesting ideas, and the entrepreneur has the fire within to put them into action. And today, with so many ideas already built, many entrepreneurs have an opportunity to build on what is already out there, like how actors can find stories they want to be a part of.

Entrepreneurial confidence is a critical factor to success as an actor as well. The world sees the many already successful actors on screen, and automatically assume their lives are abundant with happiness, success, wealth, and confidence. And while in many cases it may be true, it is not always. The Hollywood image requires maintenance as does any business. It is mentally draining to step out into a world where people want to snap photos and write tabloid articles on your every move. Success comes at a price, and the actor must decide if they are willing to pay that price.

Confidence is critical so that others feel comfortable trusting you with complex work, and trust through relationships is hugely important in this industry. It will help one create a path to success. Furthermore, one must first value themselves before others can value them. Depending on your belief in yourself, the best way is to start practicing with overcoming your limiting beliefs. Consider adopting a phrase you can say to yourself such as "I am confident, I am enough" and repeat it over and over. A lot of times negative beliefs are personal mental roadblocks that hold no truth.

Another major element of entrepreneurs is leadership and constantly working to build up those around them. Leadership has evolved to become primarily about building up people because any businessperson or artist knows that relationships between people are critical to success. Leaders can teach others their ways as mentors and create opportunities where others may succeed.

Actors often get the most recognition when it comes to film or television from the public. However, it is the producers, directors, writers, and often actors creating the films and shows, providing opportunities for more creatives, who are leading the industry. To thrive today, the most successful actors are incredibly business oriented and many form production companies. Start by giving credit where it is due and by building trust with others in the industry as an entrepreneur would in any business.

The actor provides the service of their likeness that helps to solve a problem. Producers, writers, and directors need people to fulfill very specific roles in stories. Knowing the right questions to ask can help set the actor apart. There are many problems to solve in the world, and an actor is often in a unique position to work as an actor to represent a cause they value as a spokesperson. Entrepreneurs have the desire to improve others' lives (even if it is for their benefit financially) through a product or service which is an essential element of becoming an actor as well.

The great films and television shows of the world are not just for entertainment, they relay very important messages about society, and can inspire others.

The actor can gain from an entrepreneurial perspective by spotting opportunities. Entrepreneurs see problems to be solved everywhere. This ability is a muscle that is trainable. An actor that thinks entrepreneurially can find the right place to look for their next project. And by keeping track of missed opportunities, they can revisit them. Seizing an opportunity can be as simple as giving without expecting anything back, and this can attract success.

There is a popular saying that "one must have money to make money," and there is some truth to it. However, there is also truth in the saying that "going the extra mile can yield increasing returns." Anyone can start where they are and deliver value in some way, to someone, that can help you to achieve success.

Here is a fun economic note. Greatness is earned, and a nation's wealth is based on its' productivity (Gross Domestic PRODUCT), money is simply a way to measure the amount a country produces. Success for creatives is based on the amount of art they can create, and the value others can derive from it. The passion of a creative artist itself gives tremendous value to others.

"Action," the director says, as hundreds of thousands of dollars' worth of equipment and human labor work together to capture an actor at work for a moment before the next shot. Actors already know about action in their work. It is the successful actors taking it to the next level off of the set that can help differentiates them.

Time is precious, and procrastination hurts precious time. By becoming a business, actors can narrow down what actions are most critical to their careers. It is important to know how and where to focus energy. An airplane manufacturer does not open a pizza franchise (unless there is some out-there strategy such as wanting to own pizza chains within airports). A business person often looks to move things forward, and professionals an actor works with can benefit from this skill.

Great actors are entrepreneurs because they help to create jobs. Sure, it might not be the actor directly paying the bills, but many jobs ride heavily on the ability of an actor to bring in enough attention to be worth creating a movie with over a $100MM Hollywood budget. This often requires the actor, as well as the top name directors, below the line workers, sound people, technicians and more who want to work with them as well. These massive

Hollywood projects require tremendous man/woman power, and it requires strong leaders to make them happen.

Businesses require teams large and small to make them work. Notice how many actors early in their careers continue to work with certain directors or actors later in their careers.

For example, recently I worked on a set which included actor Jim Carrey and director Michel Gondry for their 2018 show "Kidding." In 2004, these two worked together on the hit movie "Eternal Sunshine of the Spotless Mind." There are many more examples of creative teams who trust each other and build long-term relationships. These business relationships are formed on the set, and it is important for an actor to build a team for themselves off the set as well.

Modern leadership principles require the ability to recognize other contributions and work well with others for success. Notice how when an actor or producer receives an award, they always thank the others involved.

Overcoming challenges and obstacles is incredibly rewarding. Doing them consistently in the face of constant rejection is a feat. I believe actors have typical entrepreneurs beat when it comes to rejection. However, actors must be highly adaptable to the current environment which may include new technologies such as social media, or changes in workplace laws. Even though acting is glamorous and exciting, it comes with its' stresses as well. By seeing the business as it is the actor can learn how to adjust.

Great entrepreneurs are lifelong learners similar to how great actors take on more challenging roles as their careers progress, produce their self-made films, and even go on to speak for great philanthropies. Being a learner helps one spot new opportunities. It helps one become better at their craft as well as open themselves up to greater projects. Having a diversity of knowledge can help one become more likable wherever they may go. The learner may even uncover an incredible idea when trying to learn from a mentor or influencer.

While not all entrepreneurs would categorize themselves as artists, the creativity, thought, planning and execution make them very artistic in a business sense. Also, as businesses develop, they continue hiring artists such as writers, graphic designers, advertising managers and more, much like actors.

Creative thinking combined with desire and action has brought many a business and movie to life. Entrepreneurs change the world with the business they create, as actors can have a tremendous impact on the lives of many. Putting energy towards creating is where the worlds collide.

In this chapter, we looked at many analogous ways actors are already entrepreneurs, framed to help an actor see that he or she is already doing business in their everyday life. The ability is already within the actor. In the next chapter, we dive down deeper into some of the qualities and skills to succeed as an actor becoming a business.

2. Framing Your Business

With an understanding of the similarities between being an actor and what it means to become a business, let us look at certain skills that can help the actor succeed. This section helps to frame relevant business ideas as it relates to the actor. As a business develops, these factors will become more critical, even though when one starts out, one may not notice everything coming into play.

An important quality to develop is that of a great mindset. Simply improving mindset will prepare you to take the appropriate actions as you build your acting business. People want to work with people they like, and although there will always be clashing personalities, developing a great mindset will help one get along with more potential business partners and industry people. Spotting great opportunities will also come when the mind is not cluttered. One obvious method of focusing the mind is through meditation and regular exercise. Another way is to break the habit of procrastination.

If you have ever heard "most people fail because they never try," it is because their mindset was not in the right place, and realistically, a simple adjustment in thinking could have brought them great success.

The one difficult concept to understand in the arts community is that in the business community, there are three areas of focus. Businesses want to reduce their risk (of failure), to increase their revenues (or chance of success), and/or to decrease their costs.

Actors provide services as spokespeople, brand ambassadors, characters, and more. Actors sell their voice, their likeness, their name, and more. Often actors want to reduce the risk of failure by studying up more on the craft and being prepared. They may increase revenue by taking on higher paying jobs. And they may reduce costs by finding more affordable means of advertising. In any business, it is important to know what your potential clients want. This helps you even when you are facing endless rejection.

There is not always only one way to build a business or grow a career. A highly successful and famous executive shared a story about being inspired in a calligraphy class to create beautiful fonts that helped grow his business into a massive technology company valued over $1 trillion. A handful of successful actors started careers in sports entertainment as opposed to films. And concerning narrowing down to what you really want, is it truly being an actor that you want? Or is it being on television that you want to accomplish? You can be on television as a newscaster or television host, and perhaps you may even be better suited for one over the other.

Consider looking at opportunities outside the industry for inspiration. Take on a novel approach to the industry, and maybe be the first on a new media platform. Repeating the same thing over and over without any sign of success can be detrimental. Guidance can be found all over the place, and there is probably an answer to a question you have right in your email inbox right now.

As you build your business, recognize the value you bring to the table including the entertainment you can bring to people's lives. Most companies hire actors because they simply do not have people who want to provide the service of acting or they do not have the right people to pull off the necessary look. By doing a little bit of Research and Development (R&D) or Market Research, you can narrow down what industry people like to call "your type."

Deliver value by spreading meaningful messages as well and remember the actor's job could be to make people cry, laugh, or inspire massive change in the world. Eliciting emotion and influencing lives is a great responsibility, and it is your business. The stories told, the character actors portray, and the products advertised are going to influence people.

Over time, the service you give will evolve. One day you will change your hair color for a role. Another day you may become a spokesperson for global warming. As more people work with you, your past and future success will also help them. Keep improving your business and your offer. You are becoming something that people want to see. This book is about a unique business, and although the concept of business is viewed as corporate and uptight, you as a person building a brand have more flexibility.

This book contains concepts and ideas that can help one view their acting career differently. It is up to the reader to decide what information can help them, and the action to take. On set, one expected to deliver the goods when a director asks. Off the set, the actor channels their energy to either hone their skills, market their business, network, and more. Events that happen off the set are those challenges an actor goes through to experience those brief, memorable moments on set. Write down what you want, then go after it.

Like any business, the environment is always changing. Acting careers of the past are not the same as today. There are more channels and platforms and ways to get yourself out there than ever before. Technologies change, tastes change, people change, and therefore the business changes as well. Consider the hundreds of public relations, talent management, and branding teams working to gain attention for their clients.

With so much information, sometimes it is difficult to know what actions to take, and this is where a growth plan comes in even if it is not perfect. When you first start out, no one will know you, and the goal is obviously to have your business grow. Consider the ideas mentioned in this book to help you create that plan.

Furthermore, when success does come, be prepared for it. Have a good financial savings plan, and know what avenues you can market on, and prepare for positive and negative reviews. It is difficult to expect the unexpected, but at least know you can be ready for some of what is to come. A great way to prepare is to ask those who are slightly ahead of you and where you want to be, about the personal challenges they overcame. This is something you can do for any challenge you wish to overcome, not only acting. However, be aware that not everyone will be open to answering your questions. Prepare to give value first.

An actor can act as a hobby pursuing one or two community plays per year. Or they can pursue it as a business that demands growth to keep it up. Successful artists are fortunate they can live their passion, but to do so, they eventually recognize the importance of sales and marketing.

Consider what it is your business partners or clients (other actors, directors, producers) need from you and provide it to them in the form of your services. No real successful person ignores sales and marketing. Many people pay teams of people to do the sales and marketing for them.

There are many avenues for an actor to develop their business ranging from social media to commercial work to theatre. Over time, one may even consider new partnerships as skills change. Other ideas for business development include researching the news, television stations, and production companies.

When actors are not on set or preparing for a public appearance, they have what business managers might call excess capacity. Put yourself to work by preparing your next project or taking some extra initiative to reach out to potential clients. Consider all the different platforms you can use and take calculated risks with your career to gain traction. By considering other platforms to connect with an audience such as social media, you are thereby exploring new business models.

Take for example some of your favorite social media comedians, pranksters, and content creators. They amassed audiences by creating videos and doing what they are passionate about. I would even go as far as to consider the best of them brilliant marketers. Some social media stars have moved onward to work with the Hollywood's biggest names and have deals for producing their inependently created films. The point is, there are more new routes today to achieve your goals of becoming an actor.

We already mentioned the importance of teams. As your business grows, your agents, managers, and partnerships may change. More successful actors have accountants, lawyers, publicists and more.

Success comes when your team is top of the line. That is the reason people believe getting into a top agency will automatically make their careers. It is a foot in that requires continuous development of the relationship for you to thrive. Begin by valuing others more to gain greater success and create opportunities with others because the business you are in is very collaborative.

Remember that hundreds and even thousands of people are working around you to get your project to completion. Caterers, editors, marketers, producers, line producers, directors, assistant directors, extras, and more are working tirelessly to get the shots of you they need. You may not directly employ them, but their employment does depend on your ability to deliver.

As your brand grows, so does the opportunity for others you work with. One interesting philosophy I have heard is to "treat everyone as if they could potentially have an impact on your career and see how you can help them."

Actors have two major types of customers. One is the primary client who hires you for their project. The second is the massive audience of fans that watch your content. Each unique situation requires a different strategy.

Entrepreneurs and small businesses use tools to manage their customer relations and using tools such as social media and excel when you are just starting out can be helpful. Create a process or system or framework as you build your business, then try to repeat it regularly. There is a tremendous amount of trust needed when reputations and lots of money are on the line.

Like any business, reputation is critical, and as you become more ingrained in the industry, more people will know about you. The world is more connected than you might believe. Unless you are critical to the success of a project by becoming the creator, writer, and director of a project with all the finances, it might be best not to be known as a loose cannon or flake. And even then, it might be best to manage emotions except for very unique scenarios. By living by the golden rule of treating others as you would like to be treated, you can increase your chances of success.

Other important people to consider are the investors. We use the term investing loosely because of the nature of the industry. Investing in a major publicly traded studio might be a good way to "invest" in movies, but giving money to an independent producer or idea is more speculative.

Regardless of the definition, films are considered risky investments, even at the top levels of the industry. Tremendous planning and efforts are put into the top movies every year because those are what help companies grow. And it only becomes tougher with more competition and tighter budgets. Your goal is to build your business to a point where others can reduce their risk by using you in their project.

One good way to start this business venture of acting is to study some of your idols in the business. Read their stories, see what brands they promote, learn how they create production companies, and see who the teams are behind them.

Learn, not to copy, but to understand how they are building their business as role models. Some successful actors expand their entrepreneurial activities to create companies that sell other products such as water or makeup. Other successful actors might even be known to speak up for products they are personally invested in. It all has to do with business. And remember, businesses have values and how they want their products represented as well. Maintenance of your persona is a huge topic that can be discussed with a public relations expert.

It is easy to be passionate about something you love to do, and it is sometimes difficult to do the hard stuff that leads up to the fun activities. Actors and similar creatives get to create. Actors create characters often not thought of by others. They bring the visions of directors and producers to life. Learning better business principles can help an actor create a greater chance of success.

3. Assessing Risk

We all assess risk every single day. We trust that safe driving habits will reduce our risk of having an accident. A majority of the time we handle risk unconsciously and pursue activities that we know will bring us a reward. We automatically know those activities that are very low risk to reward ratio such as staying healthy.

When it comes to business, it can become a bit more complex especially in the face of competition, changes in the industry, and in many cases government regulations. Before starting out as an actor, it is beneficial to determine the risk of the business for oneself. View this risk with the perspective that it is not something to be feared, as much as it is about learning about the business to create a solid plan going in.

As we assess the risk of starting your business as an actor, it is important to remember that no matter what you are currently doing, there is some level of risk involved. The risk of happiness, the risk of reward, the risk of comfort, the risk of missing out. The business person determines which risk they are willing to take on, so let us look at a few factors.

Tens of thousands of people move to Hollywood annually in pursuit of starting their business. Compound that with the fact digital media is booming and making a video and posting it online to go viral is becoming a science. The industry is very saturated with hopeful people, and even very lucky people. These people often look just like you as well, with very similar personalities to you. There are also people who are more or less talented than you. On top of that cities are opening to the film industry across the country.

Even though everyone probably has a look-a-like somewhere out there, it is fortunate that still, no two people are alike; even twins often have differences. With this idea in mind, it is important to begin recognizing opportunities to make your name or stand out in some way. You can reduce your risk by building the necessary skills to produce and distribute your content. Looking to the digital arena of streaming media and OTT services, there is endless branding deal potential and commercial ads all over the internet.

It is also important to consider risk after you reach smaller milestones because when you feel great, it is difficult to determine where your acting skills are in the market. And if things slow down, be prepared for the emotional risk. By keeping your eyes on a bigger picture goal such as philanthropy, you can manage your expectations, so you will not be focused on only "acting." It is great to focus on only one thing such as acting, but this industry is different, and often, there are examples of highly successful actors who expand their ambitions.

In this industry, advice is abundant, and it changes from person to person. Sure, there are important standards for professionalism, and the moment you hear a standard, you will hear another offshoot story about what someone else did to succeed. To succeed, continue to master your mind and remember that getting customer feedback is easy if it is about an inanimate object you are selling, but not about yourself.

There are many catch-22s with becoming an actor too and this book is aimed to help you eliminate them by focusing on the fact it is a business. Show business is a business that deals tremendously with people. It is important to reduce the number of catch-22's you focus on and become more adaptable to the technology changes in the industry. The movies and shows of today are made differently than they were in the past. There are more possible routes to becoming successful in Media & Entertainment today than ever before.

The challenge a beginner in the industry faces is, most of Hollywood is very traditional, doing business much slower because it reduces their risk. One could even argue a lack of change creates an even higher risk of failure eventually.

Look at all the business activity happening with the top players in the industry. Multiple billion-dollar acquisitions and mergers are constantly on the news and agencies have merged. In this landscape, it is important to take the initiative and lead instead of waiting. By now you have some ideas that can help guide your approach. Take one of the ideas in this book and try to put it into action or reread a section that is useful to you. The final chapter of this book is a compilation of ideas for each chapter of this book as well.

Another way to reduce risk is to work hard and smart. The benefit for my dear reader here is that many people believe they are working very hard at their craft. Only a small number of them really are. There are ways to work with greater impact as well. Remember to work hard like any other entrepreneur or small business, and constantly move different parts of your career forward instead of waiting.

Look up some of the biggest stars over some of the past 20 years. You will notice many of them are becoming executive producers of their own independent shows and movies. These are your influencers who are not waiting around for something to happen. If you choose not to work hard and smart, prepare for the pitfalls.

This industry has an incredibly high failure rate. So does the mobile app industry, restaurant industry, publishing industry, and more. This rate is compounded by the fact the industry has relatively low barriers to entry. This may sound bad, but it helps one who truly wants success to stand out more.

There are very few at the very top of their game, and it is often easy for the average person to lose sight of the tremendous amount of work these actors put in when they first started their careers, and even now at their peak. Learn the ability to transform failures into (or lost customer because you did not book an audition) learning opportunities just as a sales team may write a report on their latest won or lost deal. Those at the top of their game are major household names that still need to protect their likeness, and you can prepare for this as well by adopting some of the lessons in this book.

Starting your business today means preparation for changing fads. Our times are moving much faster than they did for stars of the 1930's-1950's. It is the top people who understand the importance of building a business who are keeping the industry moving as well as their careers. They have survived tough times and droughts in opportunity, yet they also know how to build momentum even after a long slump. This momentum is compounded because others in the industry may also want to benefit from your momentum; even those whom you may not be associated with. Concerning those you may not be associated with, keep an eye out for potential scams and check references when possible.

If you can imagine how you might evolve your business over 30 years, then you can reduce risk. I am not saying to create an extensive 30-year plan (although it would be great albeit potentially impractical if you did). One can start looking at current entertainers and see how they have evolved their careers. Some move over to television, others started companies, others transitioned out of a different industry. Others found their path to the industry through standup comedy and improvisation troupes.

The glitz and glam of borrowed Hollywood outfits for the red carpet and beautiful people is a hyper-magnified reality. The masters in Hollywood know how to shock the mind, capture attention, and put people in complete awe through sound, sight, and emotion.

Hollywood is a cultural capital of the world. Take a moment and appreciate this before assuming that lives are suddenly filled with jets, diamonds, and parties. And surely those gifts will come at some point if this is what you desire from your pursuit. At some point, you may even get paid to make a public appearance. Know that if you choose to live in Hollywood, you are surrounded by some of the top media and entertainment professionals in the world.

If you are planning on going down the path of acting, take a look at the financial risk you are willing to take. Success is many times more likely if one can focus on a specific purpose in life. Be prepared to move and be prepared for the business upstart costs. All businesses require some investment in education, lawyers, accountants, marketing, and employees.

Becoming an actor is no different. The costs are a bit different, and monetary management is still necessary. One example is to consider the cost of living in Los Angeles to pursue your career versus another mecca for actors such as New York. New film towns are opening in places such as Texas, Georgia, Louisiana, and Seattle. Budget and plan accordingly.

Having a strong support system can also be helpful. Sometimes this requires building a completely new network of people which has become easier with social media. One difference many other businesses have that actors building businesses do not have is the ability to get a loan from a bank. Here is the thing though, banks need to give out money because loaning and investing is a major way they make money.

Here is something you can do. If you are a highly ambitious actor, come up with a strong enough business plan to convince a bank to provide you with a loan, or start a business such as a production company with a functioning budget and income. As your business grows, you can also have the support of your fans as well, who may even defend your honor when facing online criticism. Build those close business associates quickly and let that relationship bloom. At the early stages, your associates are a support system and can help with creating independent films and recording auditions.

When first starting out, depending on if you are testing the waters, or whether you truly want to be in this highly rewarding business, you will have to manage your finances. Either work a flexible job and keep testing the waters or work hard full time until you can go all in for an extended time. Success in this industry could happen either way, and focusing can only increase the opportunities. By pursuing it all in like an entrepreneur trying to find your first customers, you may uncover more chances for success.

Another factor of risk to consider is the market and opportunities. The ability to tape your own audition and email it in can be done from anywhere, and this makes people across the country viable candidates for a film. This makes understanding the business critical.

You can consider different locations to move to, and you can research production companies easier than ever before with the internet. As you evaluate the market demand for "yourself" take a look at what skills are expected of you, to increase your chances for success. Sometimes it is a simple change in look that can positively influence your career. Remember that all businesses do market research on their product.

While doing all of this, it is important to keep honing your skills. Even when entrepreneurs first build their businesses, their responsibilities continue to change over time. There are rappers starting clothing brands, and actors starting makeup brands and investing in technology companies.

Do not limit your strengths because you are so focused on doing one thing. All businesses transition as they grow. Some useful skills you can explore that might help include video production, or even learning about sales to improve your interpersonal skills. This industry is beginning to accept more diversity today.

Luck eliminates a lot of risks. It is important to see luck as something you can increase, the more you are around it. If you define lucky as "working in a restaurant and having a producer ask you to be on a television show", then put yourself in more scenarios where you work in a restaurant around producers of television shows. That is one effortless way to create more luck, and it starts first with a well-written definition.

Consider what people who are successful look for in others they would like to work with and take on those qualities. If you think luck is simply being in a movie, creaing an independent film is a step. It can be less than ten minutes. Luck can eventually come with enough effort and dedication to your business and work.

4. Deliver Value to Create Your Success

All businesses are successful because they are delivering a product or service of value to a customer. Knowing your value will be critical to your success as an actor. Knowing your business will be critical to success overall, and consistently sharing your value to others is the job. You may find success delivering value as a single character, as a brand spokesperson, as the voice of a cartoon, or some other great use of your likeness.

Before continuing further in this chapter, it is important to define what success looks like in the near and long-term. I imagine your mind works quickly and you are considering all the possibilities right now. Take a second to pause when you have a moment and write out what success means to you. Is it a spot on a hit television show? Is it landing a great commercial? In the long term, do you want awards, or are you mostly in it for the fame as a personality? There is no obligation to judge your own reasons for wanting all of this.

Make success more of a psychological mindset relating to achievement than it is about money. Success will mean different things to different people. Keep this idea in your mind and start working towards it. All successful businesses define their own goals whether it be improved customer service or improved operations.

To make the money you need to make a living off your business as an actor, study what your customers need so you can give it to them. Know that value is the worth of something. People will buy things they find valuable. It will be hard to determine your value when you first start out and remember not to undervalue yourself.

Businesses do not succeed by being free. It will be up to you to decide how your business model will work when you first start out and accept that some actors are better suited to the current markets and demands and that you will need to keep seeking customers. Know your industry, research it, and bring that extra bit of knowledge with you everywhere you go.

When it comes to making money, remember that nothing is gained without first giving. Define the exact skills you have that could be of value to someone, and keep giving, and give in the capacity of an actor as much as you can. Permission is not always necessary. And as you give, remember to ask for feedback, and measure your progress.

As an actor, you will realize all the different moving parts and personalities required for deals to move forward. Agents are on the lookout to make great deals. Producers want their movie to have box office success so they can make their money back. Other actors might even reach out to you because of your brand to team up. Casting directors' reputations depend on your ability to deliver on camera. These are just a handful of the moving pieces, and you are capable of delivering something to all of them.

Looking at directors, you are an essential part of their story. You are a part of some dream they had or vision of some world or universe. Imagine for a second you saw someone who was in your dream. That person would hold significance. You are a part of someone else's imagination, a part of their world, and as such, looks aside, you are expected to deliver what they believed this person to be.

Let us also understand all the producers on a project. The producers are people who make it so that you have a place to do your work. They keep the industry moving forward by bringing all the pieces together including financing. You are a piece of their puzzle, and it is up to you as an actor to stay at the top of minds of producers, directors, and more. The producer is essentially clearing a path so that the creatives can create.

Companies are going to the bank with the belief that your likeability and relatability are going to add to their success. Major Fortune 500 brands may want to team up with your brand to produce a commercial that they believe will appeal to their audience. These companies need faces and voices for products, and they want you because their products need ambassadors to use and market them. The commercial and advertising industry is tremendous. Every company can make a commercial, but not every company makes a movie.

In any workplace situation, imagine all of the energy put behind daily activities that are going on whether in a restaurant or a call center. On a set, people are working tirelessly to get those shots for the movie. Dozens of moving pieces are put in position to capture those special moments. These are time, energy, and money investments. There are names on the line and those relations matter.

While the top names in the industry can get away with mistakes here and there on set, it is important when starting out to be on point. The challenge as an actor is to work both the craft and the business. The trap is assuming that because one is not working on set, that there is not much one can do.

There is always work to do, connections to make, or projects for production. Keep up the passion and enthusiasm even when business is slow because cycles happen, it is a law of nature like seasons. The challenge for the actor is to be as prepared as a salesperson for a major presentation, while having the masterfully crafted product of a six-sigma operations master.

There are those clients who will work with you directly to create a project; then there is your audience. Your activities, projects, likeness, and voice are packaged into a nice presentation so the general public can enjoy entertainment. Your job is to relay messages for companies, producers, and more.

Actors may not always interact with their audience directly, and it is sometimes difficult to show gratitude while some companies may send a customer service email. A successful actor who has built a business can consider remaining creative in this aspect as well.

Capturing the attention of the audience with emotion is a team effort on set and maintaining their interest off the set is another. An audience holds tremendous value, and it is important to create ways to show gratitude.

As mentioned, content will elicit emotion. Your job is to be an entertainer whether by voice, appearance, or publicity stunts and whatever creative methods there are. The combination of your talents and the teams of people who work with you is meant to create happiness, change, sadness, and sometimes fear in others with scary movies. These emotional factors all tie into the value of the product and service you provide.

As your business grows, you may become the voice of empowerment for many. Whether you are diverse, or not, your public comments can change and influence the world. People often gain strength from movie quotes and build networks around characters. Living up to these expectations, just as you may become a successful CEO of another business, is a great and fortunate responsibility.

When businesses start out, they consider marketing, mailers, outbound calls, social media, asking for customer feedback and more. Many do this through agents, managers, and public relations representatives. Starting out, we have a great opportunity to do this through social media and build our audience with smaller budgets. And social media technology is a great way to build value both with your audience and those you may work with in the future.

Keep building the story about your business, and continue to adapt as technology changes. Eventually, you can start to hire an independent team to do all your marketing work for you. With the number of freelancers available today, you can even start hiring for yourself for just a few dollars before you become a household name.

Here is something else the top names in the industry are doing. Those who have been around for quite a while and built a tremendous reputation are creating Masterclasses, sharing autobiographies, and telling their stories to help others succeed.

The top producers hire promising employees and help them claim space in the industry. No matter where you currently are, there is something you know better than anyone else that you can use to educate others. And as your career grows, there will be more opportunities to help others as well.

Adopting children, supporting inclusion, and global warming are all causes some of the biggest stars stand for. At some point, you will reach a level of success where you can start leading greater philanthropies, and this is not something you have to wait for success to start doing. Start now by considering three issues you are willing to stand for.

Philanthropy and taking a stance on a social issue is something you can start now, and as your business becomes more successful you can accomplish even more toward that cause. Philanthropy is also a great way to stay happy and get more out of life in a mentally demanding business such as Hollywood (or maybe Bollywood, or Hong Kong) stardom.

Businesses and people succeed by giving value. Businesses that adapt to the times and deliver more value faster, better, and better suited to today's demands grow and prosper. Some even generate demand for themselves through marketing activities. The most successful actors continue to reinvest what they make. There may be factors outside of your control that have an impact on your success and knowing and sharing your value will help you maintain a positive conscience. Consider taking on worthwhile experiences such as building a side business based on your brand or even developing an acting technique and building a class around it.

Over the long term, the trickiest thing can be maintaining your passion for staying in business. Persistence of passion requires regular maintenance of physical and mental health and staying focused on your core business. How you uniquely deliver your core product is up to you. Regularly ask how you can help others, and you can find success and attract those sequels and deals.

5. Setting a Purpose

Great companies and leaders have a specific purpose. You may or may not recognize that purpose just by looking at their product. A pizza franchise, on one hand, might look like a pizza company to the public. However, the only way they can separate themselves from other pizza companies might be through a unique way of delivering that pizza through a unique value proposition such as record delivery times or customer service. On top of this unique proposition, they may have a higher purpose such as "creating better communities through meal time."

Personal development gurus, business consultants, organizations, and world leaders all know the importance of having a purpose or mission statement. Establish yours early on as it will help you keep track of your progress. As you build your career, you will start recognizing others who have similar interests whom you can team up with. Simply writing down your main goal will also set you up for success compared to many who choose not to make a choice. By setting your main goal, mission, or purpose you will know where to focus your energies for the biggest impact.

Developing a purpose will be a major guiding force for you and your business of being an actor. In a world with so many choices to make, having fewer choices can make your life that much easier. Put the energy behind the appropriate tasks, and your motivation will multiply. Without a purpose, you may begin to do anything just for the sake of doing it. Your purpose can change over time, and it is important to take the time to create one.

It is very likely that you already have personal values. You may value integrity, productivity, creativity, passion, or enthusiasm. A company will spend a tremendous amount of money for a branding consultant to help them craft values that align with their business to help them prepare for the future. These values are different than mere monetary value because they act as decision-making tools when you start getting work. And if you trust your values enough, they will eventually bring you to where you want to go.

Pursuing a career in entertainment can be very difficult simply because there is so much to lead you astray from your goals. Attention is constantly transitioning between different people. Maintaining a strong purpose to focus on will keep you going when you are uncertain. It provides you an opportunity to know that there is something to accomplish every day. The purpose helps to maximize your certainty and builds confidence.

There are many books and resources to help you find and define meaning for your own life. Simply creating a purpose will help you work towards greater fulfillment. The fact that many people do not know about writing down some purpose or mission statement means you will stand out from the rest.

Studies are showing that those who wrote down life goals before college graduation were more likely to achieve them years later. Think about how many people still wonder what their life purpose is because they have a difficult time making a choice. Pick one, stick to it, and evaluate to see if it still makes sense in the future.

To appreciate the purpose of a guiding purpose, take a look at your favorite major company and search for their mission statement. Chances are they have one available on their website. Now consider all the employees in that business that work toward that single purpose through their assigned tasks. That is energy. Energy towards your purpose is powerful. Knowing you take a step every single day is incredibly rewarding as well. Create your personalized initiatives, and become a business, then find ways to put more energy behind your work.

A mission statement can separate one business from another business that sells the same product. A technology hardware company dedicated to helping businesses adapt to change differs from a technology hardware company dedicated to helping small businesses. Knowing the power behind a purpose to work at, take five minutes to decide and choose a purpose, then write it down. There are books dedicated to helping you create an extensive purpose, and you can research them after getting started right now.

When considering a purpose, it may be helpful to add material (physical objects you wish to have like a car) or financial elements as well that is personal and kept to oneself. Your purpose can be more than simply altruistic. If your only purpose is to become rich and famous, I know you can do it, and consider the fact that many people who can fill your shoes also have this desire, and they add an extra meaningful purpose on top of it.

The purpose of your business can be more subjective as well such as creating a positive public opinion on a certain subject. The thing is, objects are easy to obtain. You can take nearly any entry-level job today to make enough to rent the very object you desire, and you will have accomplished your purpose. Then what? This is why the purpose should be more challenging, and it is ok to be about money as long as it includes some plan for its' attainment.

In consideration of the level of challenge, to be sure multi-billion dollar corporations have the luxury to save the planet by spending on philanthropy and getting great tax benefits. They can also reduce the consumption and have a huge impact. By putting a focus on costs aside, you can create a challenging enough purpose for yourself. The more challenging and rewarding, the more effort you are likely to put in daily.

Remember to celebrate the small wins and realize how they take you a step towards hitting those major milestones. It will even impact you at an unconscious level, similar to how a mission statement at a large company impacts their day to day activities between individual contributors.

All of this is information is meant to get you rolling when you are unsure of what to do. To maintain consistency, the actor must know when to separate craft from the business. Similar to how a sales team understands their product and its' benefits while having the soft skills to get the product to the public. Chances are you want to stay in the business for the long term.

How many times have you heard of the entrepreneur or inventor failing many times before finding the business or product that launched their career? Very few people are incredibly successful on the very first try.

When considering your purpose, making it about something personal will have a profound effect on you. You can keep the public statement you have for others and have your personal reasons protected in your mind. Now for "big business" purposes, there is a huge push for transparency. The idea is not to publicly say one intention but have a completely different one underneath.

The idea is to keep your personal thoughts private for obvious reasons while working toward a larger collectively beneficial goal. Similar to how a business might have a mission to "bring families together," and although employees at the company might have a different life purpose, they all work towards the same goal. There must be something to align with, which is great as you build your team or create greater personal alliances.

Your imagination is one of the most powerful things you have control over, and it has incredibly powerful outward effects as well. Great business ideas come from great people with great imaginations who continue teaming up with more great people with great imaginations. Great inventions do not come out of thin air. Great art does not magically appear.

An epiphany might occur, or a muse might inspire a piece of work after an extended amount of focused contemplation of a specific topic. It is up to you to actively use the imagination muscle to develop both your craft and business as you pursue your purpose. Apply your imagination towards imaging what it might look like to achieve your purpose down to minor details such as what your phone may look like when you are looking at the amount of money you have in your bank account. This concept of visualization has helped business leaders, athletes, and many more win in life.

Imagination is highly valued in actors. As an actor you probably imagined yourself giving an award-winning speech, interacting in a scene, or developing a character. Focus this imagination further on your purpose. Create a plan and find creative ways to take action every day.

As you get closer to or reach your goals, start to evaluate and see what you can adjust. Businesses do this through employee evaluations and customer feedback, and they change over time.

Ask yourself the right questions about your career and stick to what will positively affect your business.

It requires continued emphasis that in today's business environment and the future, adaptability is a critical skill. As an actor, you ideally can adapt yourself emotionally, physically, and mentally. Now learn the skills of adapting to business by learning more about deal structures, production, and even marketing tactics. Figure out where you failed and adjust. Continue to magnify your successes, and even try a new training method to improve your skills. Be sure to let your purpose guide you.

6. Creativity

The industry you are building a business in is filled with artists, dreamers, and creators. Show business transforms lives, creates social change, and motivates action. You know the power of media, and it is creative minds that power it. It is not enough to be a good-looking person. You are also expected to have high levels of creativity and talent.

Viewing your acting career as a business does not limit your creativity. In fact, it demands that you be more creative in your pursuits. Sometime in an actor's career, he or she may work with people who are not as artistic as say a screenwriter. Working with more logical thinkers a secondary communication skill to build and remember, the logistical, operational, logical people in this industry are dreamers too. Those who are not artists also obsess over their passions and become completely engulfed in their work at times. Dedication to the work is a critical factor of success whether you an artist or not.

The challenge to actors is not so much the creative side, as it is a reality. Dreams of putting your name on the Hollywood walk and seeing your name in the credits is the first step. The dream of mobile phone technology, landing on the moon, creating an oil business is the first step to starting it. Making these real is then the tough part once you decide upon the idea. Start making plans, even simple plans such as writing a title for a script or calling a friend to produce a project. Successful businesses plan for progress and so can you.

With a team of people, it is your job to create a reality that draws the viewer in deep enough to move them emotionally. Technology is changing the industry to the point where actors need the ability to walk through a giant green (or blue) room and make viewers believe they are in a fantasy world. The demand for creative ways of accomplishing difficult tasks like these is tremendous. That is ideally where you come in.

You can become a successful actor if you work at it and improve your skill. Know it. Hone your craft, and hone your business. Consider the concept of Research and Development in your craft as creating a better service for media.

Creativity is already one of your core strengths. This can apply to business and the art. The concepts in this book are here to help guide your thinking on the business side. No business can survive without creatives to help with solving problems, expansion, and more.

Think about writing rooms for television shows where multiple people dedicate themselves to writing multiple episodes. Think about the top superhero movies in theatres today and the value they create for the toy industry. One great story is immeasurable in value. This effect only compounds when it inspires others.

The reason why many artists exist is because they turn their creative ideas and unique perspectives and dreams into something tangible such as a statue. Being creative is not enough if no one hears about it. Business people are business people because they deliver great value through products and services, not because they leave their ideas on a sheet of paper. Hone your creativity and practice communicating the message by learning from directors and producers to hone your business skills.

More than any other job, an actor demonstrates ideas, traits, behaviors, and emotions through their appearance, body language, and voice. As an actor, realize that this is not an easy task for millions of people who may not even be comfortable being in front of a camera. Be the best voice that works with a director to help interpret a screenwriter's work.

Creativity is a trait that will continue to improve as you take on more challenging projects. On the other hand, great creativity yields huge numbers of decisions. There are tons of people in this industry who have tons of great ideas, yet some have not built the skills to decide what they want to work on and get stuck. Choose something that best works with your purpose and go with it. Your creativity is fuel, and use the ideas in this book to take decisive action as your metaphorical engine.

Your art is tremendously valuable, create your path and relentlessly put it out there. Great artists and business people do not let typical obstacles stop them. Be a leader for change. The biggest names in the industry are.

Great art is not created in a vacuum. Keeping them to yourself, unless you have the skill to develop every detail of your ideas will not do you justice. Create a team of people you can trust with your thoughts and develop them. Even Michelangelo work with a team.

Think about the greatest movies in the world. At some point, someone had to hear about the idea or read the script. It is about finding the right people to share your idea with than it is about keeping it a secret until everything is ready. And revealing the right information is a business skill that requires development.

Building strong relationships can be very tough when just starting out. Very few people will talk to someone who believes they are a nobody. Keep adding value to others lives, and you will get out of obscurity.

People with common goals and interests will meet at some point in their lives. And when this happens, synergy is created. When two or more minds combine for a common purpose, efforts are multiplied.

While it is necessary for command and control types of people in environments like the military, most businesses benefit from collective buy-in, especially true for the long-term. Therefore, a strong level of consensus for truly effective change.

As a creative, it is easy to get stuck on the ideas you come up with. And if you have the resources, money, and labor to put a plan into action, then command and control might work for you. It is important to now note that if you create a command and control environment around you, you might not ready for a business emergency. For the actor, this means since you likely are not running a business with thousands of employees, then it is important that those you work with, like you. There is a definite reason to team up with others and work collaboratively.

Have confidence in your skills. Actors are sometimes asked to work on instinct for their roles just as business people are asked to trust their gut when making decisions. Your confidence will create more confidence in those around you. Start believing in your product before others can, so sell yourself to yourself daily, especially when business is slow.

As deeply creative people, if an actor can see their problems from a business perspective, they may have an easier time solving them. While an actor might see an audition, a business person may see an audition as a way to present their product, increase their network, and find a potential future business partner. While someone hoping to become an actor might see a headshot as an intimidating expense, the business person has this as part of their marketing budget.

Business people and actors face the same challenges because, in the end, they are people too. They have cycles in business. They have to make decisions on where to put their money. They have mental stressors and fears. They have to deal with family and work with others in their jobs. Simply reframing how you see parts of your acting business can improve your rate of success and increase your likeliness of success.

As you read this book, one of the concerns might be "I can't possibly be both an artist and a business person!" First, cross out the 't to create "I can be both an artist and a business person!" Second, the ideas in this book might only seem challenging because an actors focus is typically on acting and developing unique characters, and having a business persona might seem like another task. As careers progress, the chances are that even successful actors want to find more fulfillment and business is a great route.

It is difficult to switch hats, and the fact is, we all have different personas. This is nothing unusual. Business owners take on roles as family men and women, community leaders, managers, and employees all in a single day. The concepts in this book will help you grow and have a much bigger impact in the long run.

Develop who you are artistically and non-artistically. Think of the most outrageous celebrity that pops into your mind. What color is their hair? Do they have opposing beliefs compared to the general population? Do they have all sorts of tattoos and piercings?

That celebrity purposely created that image, and the media purposely put their information out there. The ones who regularly work are also ones with great business savvy who have a great team of people to work their deals, or they are adept enough to manage at least a part of their own business.

As an actor, your creativity can help you overcome many challenges that other businesspeople may be susceptible to. You are adaptable and outgoing. You have great soft skills and can turn yourself into a new person for a movie. Allow this adaptability to carry over to help you succeed. Develop the communication skills of a great leader and prepare for the challenges ahead. After all, you can have complete control over yourself, your thoughts, and your actions.

7. Business Model

Let us spend some time to evaluate business models. We can start by keeping it simple. A business model is how you plan to make money, and this can change over time as well. Saying you want to act in movies is simple enough to get started.

To thrive, let us define the idea of a business model for actors further. There are many ways big name actors make money other than simply being in a movie. They may make most of their money up front, or from toy deals, or from DVDs. New distribution platforms are also allowing new ways for entrepreneurial content creators to make money. Consider taking a moment to speak with a knowledgeable lawyer to understand several types of contracts for entrepreneurial content creators.

Technology is causing massive shifts in show business and will continue to do so. New opportunities are all around you to make a living, and producing high-quality content is possible with a phone. While reading this chapter, start to think about the different social media platforms and how businesses are using them to make money.

I do not know what you do not know, so here are just a few ideas: branding, content development, posting, driving traffic to their product, and more. An actor has many ways to develop a unique business model to sustain and achieve success.

This book is all about reframing business concepts in a way that is understandable to any actor without any business background. These are concepts and ideas when applied to an acting career can help you pursue it more professionally. To start, define the medium you want to make money in and learn more about it.

You can consider a new social media platform or video hosting website. While examining how you will make money, you can learn about the new ways that these platforms are creating opportunities for brand deals or bringing in advertising money. There are many examples out there to model.

Here is an activity to try. Simply write out the current way you make money as an actor. Do you make money from plays or ticket sales or are you a bit more advanced with a few brand deals as you develop content independently?

Looking at your business model, dig a bit deeper, and evaluate the tools you are using, the people you work with, and even how the producers or directors you work with might make money. This is critical to evaluating the way the industry works. Take a step and try this exercise. List the top projects you have worked on to get a better visual on what is happening in your business. The point of this chapter is to help you evaluate all the diverse ways people in your industry make money in their businesses.

From here, when you have an idea of how others work, you likely have some ideas of how you can improve your career. Start to come up with a plan. This can be as simple as imagining the steps to sourcing a script, putting yourself and a few other actors in it, and finding a person to buy the package. You can even study other successful actors and see the number of projects they are always working on to consider other activities you can do.

Remember, a nation is measured on GD Product(ivity). The more you can contribute to others in the industry, the greater the chance you have for success.

I am not saying that you currently need the ability to create one major motion picture per year. Again, the whole purpose is to look at the business models of various actors. They are making money by producing independent films, making deals, getting cast in productions, appearing on commercials, video game voiceovers, television, and many other possibilities.

Take your plan step by step and break down the complexity for yourself on your terms. For example, you can evaluate that an actor in a low-budget movie with action heroes might not make big money in the theatres, but the film could become a cult classic with toy deals. At some point, you will have to evaluate whether you want to pursue this as more than a hobby-artist.

By now you are ideally brainstorming ways that actors make money. On the one hand, you can spend the rest of your career sending in submissions on a website hoping to get auditions, or you can become more proactive and apply the information in this book.

Start backward if you must. Write out the process it might take for an agent or manager to make a deal with an advertising company to put you in their next national commercial. This should take less than five minutes, and it can help you find your gaps in knowledge about your business. You may even find a better more proactive way of accomplishing your goals.

Did you know there are screenwriting books that suggest Hollywood buys stories based on historically successful formulas? Extremely creative artistic works in film are very risky for producers with reputations on the line. There have been frameworks for stories since the beginning of time just as stories all have a beginning middle and end; they have climaxes, heroes, anti-heroes, and more. And there is the framework of how a standard story progresses.

Despite every project being different in its' unique way because they are creative, the process typically stays the same. A painter may continue to use an easel with a similar brand of paint and use similar strokes, and in the end, come up with something unique. By writing down your ideas while working in this chapter, you can find what parts of your business you can repeat to increase your chance of success.

The top names in the industry often have multiple projects planned at least a year or two ahead of time. Even ambitious actors without much success yet possibly have a script or production they are planning in the future. This whole concept of submitting yourself for auditions has become much easier process-wise with all of the online platforms, but it is much more difficult to stand out.

As an artist and creative it should be easy for you to at least imagine new ways, a multitude of ways to make money in the business or at least work for yourself to promote yourself. You can use your creativity to think of innovative new models with all of the great new platforms out there. One of the reasons I mention philanthropy so often and having a cause you believe in is because it is a staple of many big-name actors. It will help you in this section with bigger picture thinking and helping others for mutual benefit.

The next thing I would like you to do is think of as many companies or businesses that offer something for free whether it be a trial, or a book, or a gift card if you sign up for their service. Many businesses give to get, and this happens all the time. Buy one get one free is another example. Look at all the entertainment some actors provide for their audience through trailers and their social media profiles.

Actors offering things for free is happening all around social media, and they do it so their fans or audience will take the time to watch their big show, commercial, or film. Some actors perform at free comedy shows while another might make a public appearance for a good cause. Know your core business whether it be comedy skits, film, or horror movies, and you may spot an opportunity to give, to grow your audience. You might even be able to expand your services in other ways such as small dinner theatres or to theme parks.

With the previous mention of free, it is important not to undervalue yourself, and this can be incredibly difficult. You may have to work for free here and there to help build your reputation. Trust your judgment and make sure to transition yourself out eventually. After all, this chapter is about finding the model you will use to make money. Perhaps you provide hours of free video content on your website because you have advertising partners who pay you to do so. That is a completely legitimate business model as well.

Here is an idea I see finding success on social media, and it is so simple but has immense potential: create a unique brand. Some people paint their nails pink, others get tattoos added or removed, and some people make sex tapes. There was a famous actor who once said something along the lines of "I do not have multiple personalities. I am just the owner of my stage persona." I am not saying do anything you are uncomfortable with. You may have to get creative though.

Even in the world of acting, having a conservative look might bring more opportunities than in the world of rock stars. However, some unique personalities who chose to stand out have become successful and get acting projects because of their success. There are also opportunities to create personas on social media for marketing while maintaining your squeaky-clean record.

Another question to ponder is whether to incorporate or not. At early stages, the real benefit of incorporating is to protect your likeness, own your intellectual property, and get used to owning a business entity such as an LLC. You may notice that many top producers and actors do in fact own their own production companies. It is something you may not need early on although it is a great route to consider when moving into bigger and better deals. There are many affordable resources to consult with a lawyer and accountant for this purpose.

Let us look at operations for now, or what makes your business work on a daily basis. As an actor, your physical product must be top notch. This book is not meant to help discuss the craft of acting or acting technicalities. Without a good product or if you fail to provide the service expected of you, you have no business. There are many lucky actors out there who might get a break without training, and that is fantastic, but in reality, going through some training will help increase your opportunities. Do not let the highly lucky few influence your belief of what truly happens in our industry.

Aside from your acting skills, your other business-related operations include figuring out how to sell and market, managing relationships, and even technical activities such as social media or website management. If you produce independent projects, it is necessary to understand a bit of those operations as well. Perhaps your agent might even be a part of your operations. By framing these different aspects of your business operation, you now have a much different perspective of the business than other actors.

Businesses do not grow without sales. Actors with an audience increase the chance of a movie becoming successful. Actors who deliver great service get called in again for more auditions. On the one hand, auditions can be viewed as a very different type of sales pitch. You can learn about your customer's needs by reading the breakdown and even go as far as to study the producers. Define your sales process of what it takes to go from not having an audition, to booking work.

We mentioned earlier that there are a few types of buyers. There are those who make a contract with you to use your likeness, voice and more. Then there are those who tune in to your show or buy tickets to one of your movies. There is a desire to see you perform. Remember all of the work required to capture that one brief moment of you and the people who will admire you. By knowing a bit more about this audience, you can learn to uncover more opportunities by appealing to them through platforms such as social media.

Looking more in depth to those who contract with you, they will require deeper relationships. These are clients as much as they are friends and business partners. Sometimes they are shooting a commercial and only want to sell a product that has nothing to do with you. Sometimes they are up and coming producers who might use you for a project in the future. Understand what their different expectations are and build relationships that way. Another exercise here is to break down the different roles and decision-making capabilities of casting directors, producers, directors, and even branding agencies. This activity can help you manage your sales and marketing.

At some point, you may become known for the way you approach the business. Perhaps you might become known as "Hollywood's Princess" or "Hollywood's Bad Boy." This persona might come about organically, or because of certain repeated public relations campaigns or projects you do. As you gain mastery over your craft, keep mastering your business model for more income. If you do lots of commercials, keep on mastering your relationships with commercial producers. If you are working on short films, find ways to help producers take their project to the next level. By applying all of these principles, you "increase your luck."

I am about to share with you wisdom that has been true since the beginning of time. Action is critical to your success. Anything that exists in your mind which has not been put into a physical form whether it be written, recorded, created, or some form of action, is essentially non-existent as far as anyone else is concerned. Even taking one of the ideas in this book that you valued, and rewriting it on paper can help you move forward. You can call a friend or make a post on social media. Another idea is to write a title for a script or write a synopsis for a dream you wish to turn into a movie. Maybe you are ready to simply cold call producers. You can even send me an email.

8. Money Management

Wherever you are in your career, it is hugely important to have a financial plan as well as budgets. The one problem with the whole concept of acting and auditioning today is there is a lot put to chance (especially for the early stages). For any single project posted online, there are hundreds if not thousands of people who submit for an audition. It is difficult to create a solid financial plan when your income might be unpredictable. This book is here in part to help you create a more predictable stream of income by viewing your services more business-like.

Starting with our previous chapter, let us examine your business model. Continue to reference those ideas you came up with in the previous chapter. As you move forward, keep staying on track of the happenings throughout your process. Notice that it does not always have to be a waiting game, and there are opportunities to become more proactive, and you now have the skill to recognize them as an actor building a business. Perhaps you may even be able to start spotting an investor or two.

When it comes to financing a business, traditional banks are an option as well as a whole multitude of services looking to sell their money to profitable businesses. Unfortunately, it would be very difficult for an actor to benefit from these resources unless they had a side business plan to launch a production company or branded product. Other ways to obtain financing is through crowdfunding, seeking a producer who wants to invest and selling advertising space.

We will talk specifically about basic money management skills. These are likely rules you have heard before and are working hard to put them into action. However, one cannot know, what they do not know, and I do not know, what you do not know. Simple guidelines include making sure to pay off all debt as soon as possible, spend less than you are making, let your money work for you, find a certified advisor to speak with, and learn what it is you truly want. Learning about what you truly want is critical because, for most people, it is not money they want, but what comes with money that they want.

One great place to learn about money management is in books. I can only tell you so much in this chapter about how to manage your money better. The great thing about books by experts is they provide solutions for any problem you may have, whether that is getting out of debt, increasing your income, or simply learning how to manage the money you are making better. When looking at the actor, many can get stuck in jobs they completely dislike for far too long in hopes of waiting for that golden opportunity.

Seek expert advice by reading personal development books, and ways to build businesses around your passion. If acting is a passion, there is no reason you cannot be on camera every single day to build your audience. While reading this chapter, you can consider your other passions as well as to include horseback riding, making music, or even computer graphic design. These can be turned into jobs you like if you are having difficulty maintaining an acting career.

One scary thing many actors start out with after college is too much debt. I will not provide advice on this as there are great advisors on call waiting to help you. There are a tremendous amount of resources out there to help you understand it better. On the other hand, when it comes to business, all companies have debts, and debt is not something to be feared. The problem is also typically more about finding a higher income opportunity than it is about struggling with debt. Increase your financial education, manage your finances, and understand there is a light at the end of the tunnel.

For anyone starting out in any business, they need a proof of concept. As an actor, if you are starting out, you are regularly asked to provide proof of your service and the popularity of it. This proof of concept is a combination of your talent and way of building relationships in the industry. While an inventor might have to develop a model of their new gadget, you must show the industry professionals that you are ready for the general audience. It is through proving yourself that you can demonstrate your value, find projects, and start working more.

By applying this information, you are positioning yourself for greater success. You are creating a strong foundation upon which to build an acting career. Certain artists may play very similar roles throughout their careers. Other actors may play very different roles known because of their ability to portray a range of characters. However, both those actors are finding ways to repeat their method of delivering their service.

The big challenge is because of the project-like nature of films. Improving operations on an assembly line for a car is done with fancy operational management techniques such as Six Sigma. Unfortunately, these techniques are not as easily applied to project-oriented businesses such as filmmaking and construction.

If examine a few successful actors over the course of their careers, we will notice how their skills improve. Their wardrobes are finer over time and the types of films they star in become better. This is an example of the actor improving the quality of their brand over time, and this is a possibility for any actor just starting out. Furthermore, if you can improve your people skills, you can improve your ability to succeed in this business as well.

Relationships are critical. Think of it this way, if you want to start a movie theatre business, would you rather have a $1,000,000 investment from someone who knows nothing about that business or would you rather have $100,000 investment from a retired executive of a global theatre chain who also wants to be a full-time board member and advisor? This made up scenario is meant to highlight the importance and value of relationships.

The relationships you have in the business help to reduce the risk for people who are putting in their time, effort, and money. This is true for all successful businesspeople and businesses. Ask any high-level executive and ask them about the importance of relationships. The challenge for any entrepreneur includes building relationships with employees while also creating a relationship between the company and your customers. For the actor, the company and products are the same.

Risk reduction is why there are different lists (a list, b list, etc...) for actors. A movie producer can increase the success of a film simply by hiring a list actors. Sure, there are other factors involved such as story, directing ability, and more, and it is important to start understanding this concept and apply it to your work. It will also help ease disappointment when you are not cast.

The beauty and challenge of your business is the fact that art is subjective, and your service as an actor is subject to opinion as well. While commodity products such as paper or bananas can be bought with very little consideration, your skill as an artist is not as easy to measure. You are not a commodity. You are a thriving, living, breathing artist and therefore can become as valuable as you decide depending on how effectively you work. The hard part in today's huge digital sea is keeping yourself in front of the right people.

To manage money, you must have some available. Whether you decide to put your savings behind an acting career or you want to have two jobs while going to auditions is up to you how you decide to manage your finances. Remember that all businesses have startup costs, and while you may complain about the cost of headshots, there is a man or woman out there trying to privatize space travel. Fortunately for you, the barriers to entry as an actor are low compared to many other highly regulated industries.

After you have understood more about debt and considered ways you are going to make a living as an actor, start planning for growth. If you stay dedicated to your business long enough, your network will grow, and your quality of projects will increase. There is a common practice among gurus who help people succeed, and that is to estimate the amount of money you want and imagine and write out how that money is to be allocated.

Most high net worth people do not have all of their millions of dollars sitting in a single bank account. That is incredibly risky as they lose out to inflation. Take this practice of imagining how much money you want, then allocate it accordingly. If you want a total net worth of $3,289,476, then imagine where all that money will be. Perhaps you might have a percentage in the bank, a percentage tied up in your home (or multiple), some stock investments, and maybe even your own production company. Then start coming up with ideas of how to reach this status. Expect that you will thrive as an actor.

This one fact cannot be discussed enough: limit your expenses if you are not where you want to be. Keep putting your finances toward your career whether it is for marketing campaigns, or improving your operations, or entrepreneurial projects. You can even pay yourself by taking a day off from work to produce videos from your phone. Understand what it is you want and figure out how to separate business from pleasure. Soon enough, somewhere down the road, you will find all the pleasure you want, and it may even be closer than you think.

After personal expenses, chances are you are not getting traditional financing, so your expenses will likely become your business expenses. Consult an accountant to determine what constitutes a business expense and personal expense. At the time of writing this book, many new laws are impacting the way these are perceived. Spend money on honing your operations and increasing your network or education as these are yours for good. A job can be taken away, but your relationships and knowledge cannot. Measure what is working, and be prepared for change as you become more successful.

The major reason for applying the concepts in this book is to prepare for the success you seek as an actor. Very few things are ever only about money. A wealthy person may spend millions on a precious painting but be opposed to buying a new pair of shoes until they are worn down. Even a ruthless executive is not worried about money because of money itself. Instead, they are more likely worried because they could lose relationships, power, and freedom.

As you study new ways of managing your money, remember the power of relationships which you can start building right now. Sure, some difficult to access people might cost more to reach, but what kind of value would you have if you knew every major executive in the industry? You are who you surround yourself with. Manage your money because you must and get started on building those relationships that are much more valuable.

9. Your Team

This book has mentioned the importance of people and relationships multiple times. The way you work with others and your ability to grow your professional network will impact your ability to succeed. You are the CEO of your own business and must develop your network of business partners. While regular businesses have Chief Executive Officers, Chief Operating Officers, Chief Marketing Officers, Chief Financial Officers, and more people on their board, most smaller business entrepreneurs function in many of those roles by themselves.

As an actor, you may want to reimagine the idea of how traditional company teams are built and this book is here to help. Looking at the leaders in entertainment, you will find they have agents, publicists, lawyers, managers, accountants, and more. Although they may be hired externally on a per-need basis as opposed to bringing them on as an employee, these people are still crucial to success. It is possible that you may become a big enough name that you will want an in-house team managing your business. Our industry is fueled by independent contractors and outsourced services ready to help you.

Understand that the people who you bring into your circle are people who you are working with for both of your benefits. Outside of your business, you may even want to create a mastermind group. This is a group as described by many success gurus as a team of people who work together for a common benefit. This group can start as simply as with your significant other, or you can work tirelessly to find the right person with whom you can accomplish your goals. The key factor is to make sure your goals align, and that you work well together.

This chapter is critical for success in business and could be one of the first chapters of this book. It was included in the middle because my goal was to frame the concepts in this book early on and dig deeper as we go. This chapter is more effective after understanding the purpose of this book and examining your methods of operation.

When assessing your potential, it is important to realize all that is at stake for those around you. Your co-stars likely have similar goals to yours, and it would be nicer to work in harmony with them than in conflict. While it might seem like money is behind these projects, the truth is, it is the energy of the passionate people behind films and television shows that moves them forward. Your career can become much bigger than you ever expected and let us appreciate that potential now.

Spending time on a set is beautiful. At any one time, depending on the size of the project, you can have dozens of people working to capture one special moment when all activity off the camera ceases. This activity is an incredible alignment of energy put forth to create a successful film, commercial, or television show. Each moving person on set is working toward a definite common goal.

It is this harmonious effort you must align yourself with off the set to move forward in your business. When working with agents, partners, managers, casting directors, and producers, you must become aligned to a specific goal.

With every team, it is also important to recognize the wet blanket, or person whose job it is to find the potential pitfalls of an idea and differentiate them from a person who is negative all the time for no reason. If you are the negative person, you may want to figure out how to be seen as an emergency planner, and not the person who brings the rest down. Creating positive synergy amongst your team is crucial.

One of the biggest difficulties when it comes to building relationships rests in the hands of communication. With the internet and texting, it is so easy to misunderstand and disregard. Communication requires both recipient and sender to interpret a message in the way it was meant to be said.

Stories are communicated incredibly well through the big screen, yet this is not truly reflective of how it happens in real life. Whether communication happens through calls, emails, or social media, there are different skills required for all of those mediums. And they can be used to strengthen relationships. With so many ways to stay in touch, there is no reason to not maintain a clear open line with your most important relationships and beyond.

Another important factor to consider when building your team is establishing your strengths and weaknesses. Learn about yourself and your weaknesses or things you do not want to do as you learn to team up with others. Actors do not critically need to know how to write a screenplay, and they do not need to know how to operate a camera, nor do they need to know how to create a SWOT (Strength, Weakness, Opportunity, Threat) analysis for their business. These can all be helpful skills, but bringing together the right people who can help with these concepts is the important idea.

Knowing a little bit about each these skills can help improve career outlook. An actor who is also an executive producer who is also assertive enough to write their own content has tremendous value. Numerous actors started their careers by producing the scripts they wrote for themselves. At the start, most actors have to learn to do a lot by themselves. By focusing on the end goal, and the opportunity to do what you love, all tasks can become easy. You may not find a Hollywood agent or manager that is going to work their tail off for your success for many years. Continue working towards hiring that person and forming that professional relationship.

With so many moving pieces, it can be easy to lose touch with those working with you. Casting directors, producers, and directors may have success riding on your ability. The camera operator, gaffer, line producer, and crafty team are also working with you. I want to help categorize this concept for you.

Let us evaluate two separate groups of people on your team. One consists of your advisors, mentors, business partners, and board members who take a percentage of what you make. These are the people with the most at stake in the project. They can include managers, publicists, lawyers, casting directors and closely partnered producers or directors.

The second group consists of those who will work alongside you during a project such as the crafty team, wardrobe, set designers, and more. These are all important jobs and people and the interactions will be different.

While group one participates in the bigger picture and works with you long term to create a mutually beneficial relationship, the second group is part of your success at the time, and possibly in the future. Understanding this difference is important because as a leader, others have to want to work with you. Furthermore, you may want to prepare to communicate your needs to both categories of business associates.

Another popular way to grow your team is by bringing on mentors. While they may not directly impact your success by doing work tasks for your benefit, they can provide critical information. These can even be advisors from outside the industry, but with specific expertise on a topic such as marketing or social media. You can call them consultants, advisors, or mentors.

The other thing to recognize about mentors is they can be from anywhere ranging from a blogger you follow to a celebrity whose autobiography you have read, to an experienced industry professional you pay to mentor you. It is up to you to decide what you can afford or how you will go about obtaining mentors. Do not be scared to spend money on a mentor. Realize that coaching, consulting, and advising is a completely legitimate business. Proceed with caution, and make sure you research anyone before giving them anything.

We had an entire chapter on what it means to give value. People want to work with people who can work with them for mutual benefit. You may encounter people who are more selfish, and it is important to watch out for them, but remember to attract to yourself those who you want to work with, by being a person you want to work with.

Give more and success will come because prosperity comes from productivity. You can provide some service to people even if it is as simple as sharing an article that can help their business grow. Providing a service, sometimes for free feels good as well. Even when a celebrity is not working, they are often still connecting with their audience via social media or planning their next project. I am not saying never to take a vacation. I am saying that there are a series of attainable steps you can take to increase your opportunities.

Actors and celebrities carry a tremendous weight on their shoulders. The lives they live are dreams for many. This weight can often even drive actors down a path they would not wish upon themselves if they realized what was happening to them. By realizing your potential as a leader, you can be your best. By being your best, more people will want to join your team or have you join theirs. There is a long career ahead, and let it be a healthy prosperous one.

We will end with an exercise you can try to show that the concept of a team happens even though actors typically do not recognize it. Consider the top movie franchises to include superhero and science fiction movies. List the actors who appear in more than one of these movies. There is a team of actors right there. And more than likely, when you view the credits, you may find even more names in common amongst the movies.

Another thing to do is research the agents and managers behind some of Hollywood's top working actors. Notice that many actors who work in movies may be from the same agency. This is not a coincidence. Team players support their teammates.

One final example I will ask you to consider is to look at earlier movies of your favorite actors. Even if the film is not a franchise, you may notice that some actors work together later on in their careers, and in other movies with the same directors. This again is because of the importance of building relationships and a team which can change over time as well.

10. Growing Your Business

The interesting thing about becoming a business as an actor is the fact that one single booking can skyrocket a person's career. This is slightly different than other small business entrepreneurs because small business entrepreneurs find ways to make their business globally known in different ways. They must find financing to fund their marketing campaigns, and improve their operations, and please shareholders over time.

The illusion is the assumption that the actor just suddenly became successful because they got lucky. This is far from the case. More often than not, an actor has done a tremendous amount of work and gone through a tremendous amount of failure and rejection before being in their box office hit. Yes, there are scenarios where an actor had a career since childhood, but to maintain careers over a long time, they eventually learn to manage their business well. They continue to hone their skills, build relationships, and improve what they do.

Many actors have success, then fall out of the spotlight sometimes by choice, sometimes because they have a difficult time finding more roles in the tough Hollywood landscape. Then some actors have very long-term careers and manage to stay relevant because they work with incredible people and manage their time and money for long-term growth.

The entertainment industry is ever evolving, especially as technology completely changes society and the way we consume content. And today, everyone wants a piece of the motion picture industry whether it be distribution, production, film financing, or simply using it as a tool to keep eyes on their platform. We are in an exciting time of great opportunity. There is more great content than any person can reasonably consume, and the industry is filled with incredibly passionate people. Outside of television or movies, digital advertising budgets are also providing a tremendous opportunity for commercial work.

There is no time like now to push yourself to another level. And with the level of competition out there today, there is no excuse not to. As you begin to work more, there are even opportunities to sustain a living by sharing what you have learned. Keep challenging yourself by growing your core network of people and become more fulfilled in your pursuits in your wonderful business.

There is an unfortunate number of known artists and business people who ended up broke, alone, and dependent. Some of them were even considered great. If you want to live comfortably while doing what you love, remember the vital importance of how sales grow your business. There are ways to stand out and sell your services and not be stuck in the masses of people who want to try to be an actor. After all, you know now the importance of becoming a business.

Consider learning a little bit about the sales process. The way business is done at the very top is not the way you are doing business. A list stars do not go to cattle calls. This does not mean you should never go to a massive audition with dozens of people who look like you if you are not an A-lister. That is an opportunity to perform. What this means is that your business changes over time, and it becomes a responsibility to recognize new opportunities to thrive.

As an actor, you can experiment with your marketing. While there is a possibility of getting categorized as a type of actor, there are numerous examples of comedians transitioning to drama and actors transitioning out of the film industry. There are also reverse examples where actors were told they could never find success outside of their category, and they went on to prove themselves. Some notable examples include Jennifer Aniston, Meryl Streep, and a more controversial Traci Lords. Change happens.

With marketing, you have more opportunity today to connect with people who can help your career than ever before. Make it your duty to share your art with the world. Marketing does not have to be scary. Eventually, you can hire a publicist to help, and you might be amazed by the campaigns some publicists create.

As you grow your business, your tactics will change, and your relationships will change. I am not saying they must change. I am simply saying be open to the idea that it could happen. Be open to new business partnerships and learn from mistakes. Explore new friendships that are more supportive of your career because changing your team can help launch your business.

One very well known technology company fired their CEO, and then re-hired him many years later to help them come out of financial turmoil. This is not so much about "not burning bridges" as much as it is about maintaining the relationships that matter most. Perhaps it might even be you that is holding someone else back.

After a success or two, you might find that your acting career hits a slow period. Some very adaptable entertainers manage to stay in the public eye throughout their careers. Trends and fan tastes will change over time. Be aware that all businesses go through cycles, and when some recognize that their business is having some tough times, they make critical changes. Remember to manage your money appropriately so that you can prepare for the downtime.

Sooner or later, you will have the funding to be an executive producer on your own project. Some might even say this is a necessity at later stages of successful careers. Remember to separate your different expenses and put some towards future projects. As you begin spending your money from a business perspective, you can evaluate the return on investment from a business expense such as a headshot. If you just landed a major commercial or television show, it might be good to invest some of those business earnings into a publicist.

Another important consideration as you transition into higher quality work is how you will protect your intellectual property.

There are ways to protect your likeness, and you will likely want to only work with the most professional productions as your career progresses. There are resources for you such as joining an actors union. Over time, you will have an easier time determining your tremendous worth. The projects you do today will have value later on, should your career take off.

The idea of creating a production company may also cross your mind as you grow your audience. You can use this to protect your assets as well as to develop projects in the future. There are resources all over the web that can help you get an LLC set up very quickly for a reasonable price.

With great growth come great pains. Huge technology companies often started as small websites or as ideas. Actors who are household names sometimes started as actors in small local theatres. Over time, they had to adapt to becoming more successful, and managing new relationships, opportunities, and fans. This is not an easy obstacle. Tie this in with the changing demands of the industry and mental preparation for incredible popularity one year, and the decline a few years later.

In preparation for these changes remember the successful stars and businesses of today are not what they were 10, 15, or even 20 years ago. Simply recognize that your brand must transform with the times. Even who you decide to team up with and hire could change. You will work with bigger names, and others will continue to expect more from you. And soon enough, you will be more focused on creation rather than seeking opportunities to do so.

Social media has made it possible for people around the world to build a name for themselves without the huge Hollywood budgets. You can do this by starting with honing in on what you want. Practice visualizing what your assets and partners look like. This will help you to even write your own stories in the future. Visualization has a profound effect when done correctly and imagine everything from how you will travel to how the way you do business will look a year from now.

As you start evaluating the concepts in this book, remember your relationships. Either find someone who is great at managing your business relationships, or you must be incredible at it yourself. Start considering a list of people you have worked with in the past because your brand will affect them in the future. This is not about managing the people around you as much as it is about remembering your potential stakeholders as any business would.

If you start paying more attention to the news, you will notice information about celebrities opening restaurants, investing, and selling real estate. This is proof that either someone is managing their business for them, or they are doing it themselves. There are celebrities opening clothing lines, makeup brands, and others focusing strictly on producing more iconic movies. The concepts in this book will help you recognize what it means to become a business.

11. Being Loved

This chapter is more humanistic than business. There is a popular quote, "would you rather be loved, or feared." And this quote does not apply to an actor's business because they are not ancient medieval rulers. This may be one of the tougher to grasp concepts which I left for last, because of the nature of the word "love."

Do not confuse the giving or receiving of love with becoming a pawn. It is possible to be loved and demand what you need or want from life at the same time. It is also possible to become a brand of artist that touches on the darker, edgier, or tougher sides of life and be loved.

Yes, as an actor, you can potentially wield significant power and have tremendous influence. However, your goal is to build an audience, not scare them away. There are cases of celebrities who show lack of gratitude for whatever reason, or they may have outbursts, and that can be acceptable because we are all human but remember to recognize when it can drastically hurt your career or worse, others.

We can all use and share more love. Even looking from a strictly business perspective, to stay in business, your customers must love your product. And for this industry, that product or service just so happens to be you. There are numerous platforms and opportunities for the actor to engage with their audience today and reciprocate. This is not saying that an actor can stay in contact with tens of millions of individual fans on a daily basis. What I am saying is to reciprocate when the opportunity lends itself, and there are more opportunities today. The world can use positive change, and everyone can easily show appreciation to others.

Emotional intelligence is a popular word thrown around because of the generalization that corporate leaders are assumed to have low emotional intelligence. The type of leadership necessary to lead a business has changed over the decades, and emotional intelligence is incredibly important.

As an actor, chances are you are more in tune emotionally than the average person. This connection is a unique ability to connect with others in your craft and non-artistically. Now it only requires that you seek out those you align with best. This will continue to be a critical skill as the industry becomes more diverse.

Without leadership skills, you may as well maintain a desk job as you continue to follow the whims of others. I am not saying you have to lead a revolution or be a globally renowned activist. Leadership skills will help you accomplish more with less energy. A good leader can move mountains and create positive change. While everyone works for someone (even a CEO answers to a board of directors), the leader is responsible for managing self and helping grow those who work with them.

As technology becomes a greater part of our lives (as if it was not already) soft skills will continue to grow in importance as well. By learning about what motivates others, you can help them accomplish their goals, and eventually your own. Through self-evaluation, you can learn to become an even more effective actor. These concepts work in synergy.

When your business is filled with love and passion, you will have plenty of tolerance, and this is a great characteristic that will help you long term. This includes appreciating others experiences in life and looking past your differences, to the similarities that can bring you together. The industry has become too big for narrow minds which limit the creative potential of others.

Another interesting business quote along the lines of "if what you are doing is working, you are falling behind." While this may not be the best quote to live your life by, there is some truth to it. Businesses that were crucial in defining American industries had to adapt to tremendous change over the years. Technology is completely evolving the way people work, live, and make decisions. This goes for actors as well.

Actors had to adapt to new technologies and the incredibly fast pace that movies are made compared to even 20 years ago. Technology opens up opportunity but also creates a challenge for those who are not ready and stuck in old ways, but it is an easy fix for the latter group. There are even entertainers who work solely on social media platforms that are building massive careers with tremendous representation.

Simply reading this book means you eventually want to be more than just another actor. If you keep at it, you may or may not be a household name, but chances are you will be recognized in some groups as reliable hard-working grade a talent. The higher the ranks you reach, the more opportunities you have to grow your business and give. If acting is your dream job, plan for success.

There are very few coworker relationships that are close to what actor's experience besides maybe the few lives that epic stories are developed from. As salespeople learn to do business with executives of big companies and financial managers must learn to work with high net worth people, the actor must also learn to work with other brands as big as themselves at some point.

An actor will even develop deep, intense emotions (positive and negative) toward their co-stars as required by a scene or director. Actors are trained to make these emotions real, and not "act them." Therefore, emotional management becomes an even more critical skill if this is the path you wish to go down.

Some fans may love you to the point of tears, while in the bigger picture, your career flows in cycles depending on your management. Keeping a great attitude, although difficult while portraying certain roles, will help you be loved longer.

Another aspect of being loved and appreciated in the industry is effective communication. On the one hand, you must be great at working with your co-stars and directors and producers. On the other, you might be expected to communicate your challenges with the public relations manager on how to communicate with the mass public.

Asking good questions and working with people who ask good questions is a simple skill to have to improve communication skills. And here is a question to think about: what if everyone you were in contact with was an important person? How could that change your life? Simply show you care, demonstrate gratitude, and be prepared.

It is a simple concept. The more people love you, the more work you will likely get. If people have no clue who you are or do not enjoy being around you, they cannot work with you, or they will try to avoid you. We are not saying to be a teddy bear that makes no demands or does not stand their ground when necessary. At some point, you may have to stand up against someone that is not so caring. It can be difficult as an actor to be loved and do business. That is why considering the ideas in this book can be so beneficial.

You can be loved as a feared character such as villains or monsters for example. You can ask for what you need from others as you gain more of that privilege. You might even make extraordinary requests that are bizarre as long as you do not infringe on the rights of others. You might even become successful enough that your power and money seem endless. Simply remember that in the long run, working to be loved is a great way to continue long-term success.

People will always remember how they felt around you because emotion is a powerful way to create a memory good or bad. By focusing on getting you and your product loved by your fans and those you worked with, your business can grow. Remember this: aside from the very few stories of successful business dictators, it is possible to lead and have people follow you because you know what you are doing. People want to work with leaders. It is human nature. Do this, and you can be rewarded with more of the work you are passionate about doing.

Another major challenge for the actor is to be a leader, grow their business, and be loved. Business people make incredibly challenging people decisions that can change the life of the other person for better or worse. Many great business people helped others build their careers as well. While you may not be in a position currently to promote anyone to a lead role in a television show, there are things you can do right now to help others improve what they are doing.

I am not saying to give out unsolicited advice. You can give out advice simply by sharing great stories whether written by you or others. Succeed on good terms with others, and you will have an easier time climbing the mountain. While not everyone you help will reciprocate the favor, building trust is critical early on, and the future could hold many wonderful surprises.

At the beginning of this chapter, we mentioned the potential conflict of interpretation of the word love and how it can associate with weakness when it comes to doing business. Remember that even some of the most controversial rappers and metal bands received and gave love to their fans. Their art will be remembered and appreciated for the many days ahead.

Some artists were known to be very difficult to work with and required incredible finesse by the managers and producers to handle. But also notice that some of the same people create families, great businesses, and more later on in their careers. It is about creating love for the best version of your product and service available.

If you are completely against the system and can create love amongst a massive group of followers without the system, creating positive change can help create a longer-term career. With all art, be loved for what you do, because sometimes, there is more on the line than just oneself including business partners and friends.

Now moving back to business, let us consider the cost of constantly getting negative attention. Unless this is what you specifically want (and some people might and still get a great following), we can consider the cost of a PR campaign to make your brand likable again. The media will have a big day when they get a juicy story that can ruin a reputation. Let the media work with you, not against you.

No matter how hard you work to create your business that people will love, there will always be someone who does not love it. This can be a difficult thing to accept for many if you follow the news or internet too much. There may be people who speak poorly of you, and others may speak very highly of you. Be sure to find advisors or consultants you can trust to help you build your business as well and they can help you separate the fact from fiction. Because if people truly do not want to work with you for whatever reason, it is important to know about it. And of course, a bit of humor never hurts. Have fun.

12. Keep Learning

Most successful business people (if not all) are always learning. The value of "always learning" is also a part of many successful companies. Business people are learning about economic changes, new technology, opportunities, products, services, and about ways to improve their own business. Even successful people who choose not to attend traditional schooling learned throughout their lives in other ways and here are some aspects of your business you can learn very easily.

To spot opportunities to grow your business, research what is changing in the industry. There is technology that allows you to build a fan base simply by liking each other's photos. There are cameras attached to our phones that allow you to share anything you want to say with the world at any given moment. By learning to use these tools effectively, you can grow your business or create it from scratch like no other time before.

Keep developing the skills you are good at. Many people find acting careers simply were not right for them and eventually leave the industry. The esteemed United States President Ronald Reagan (along with his wife Nancy) was an actor earlier in his career and bodybuilder turned actor Arnold Schwarzenegger eventually governed California.

By remembering what you enjoy doing outside of acting, you can maintain greater focus when you do work on it. The beauty of acting is the project like the nature of work that allows you to travel and enjoy some luxuries many corporate employees do not. You can often even use your skills to enhance your service. Stay up to date with what you enjoy doing and be happy.

Very few people have the luxury to explore the many riches and emotions of life that actors do. Look around and find ways to grow your experiences that can help you spot opportunities. By broadening your horizons, you can become more resourceful and grow your talents. Keep moving forward and grow.

One skill I kept learning about during my MBA program and my career as a salesperson was the ability to ask good questions. The only way to learn something new is to find out what you do not know, and you do not know what you do not know. When dealing with any person or topic, if we do not ask questions, we can only but learn what is at the surface. And to build better relationships, we must dig deeper.

If you ever have a chance to work in a big company or dig deep into an analytics software, you will see that the world runs on information. Technology companies become successful because of how they manage and use information. Now you are no machine, but the more information you can know, the more chances you have to "get another lucky break."

The chapters throughout this book contain thoughts and ideas that you can apply to your work. It may work today, or it may be more useful sometime in the future. Just as you may adopt new ideas from this book, you can continue to do so by seeking other resources. There is plenty of free material on the internet as well. And greater than free material is feedback from those close to you. All that takes is a call or message. Getting a new fresh opinion could completely improve the way you work.

The inspiration for this book came about through much reading and studying of related topics. I have found reading to be an incredibly affordable way to learn from the best. These resources are easily found in libraries, and plenty of the best ideas in books are sometimes repeated in online articles. After taking time to read, you can reapply the learnings in your own words. We all interpret things differently anyway.

I read concepts completely unrelated to acting and found ways to apply them to this book. You can do the same for your business by finding topics you enjoy online and subscribing to the writer's newsletters. The internet has closed the gap required to interact with the people you want to meet, so be sure to take advantage of that.

Another great resource for in-person networking and development of your business is through seminars and panels. You can potentially seem like you are everywhere online and in person. It can take time to build relationships, and certain events can help you more in this area depending on your experience. Even if a person cannot help you, perhaps you can help them, or find a friend who they can help and vice versa.

One other major benefit of face to face interactions is the compounding effect of working with like-minded individuals. And it is very likely that people at these events are where you want to be. Find them and connect.

There are a few stories of actors who claim to have never taken an acting class, or actors who were discovered while working in a restaurant. Chances are more likely that the greatest actors invested tremendously in their careers at some point. They trained their bodies, minds, voices, and more. It is not always just about acting that can get you where you need to be, because there is a lot of talent out there.

Many acting classes are developed to help an actor build certain habits they never even knew existed for working actors. Habits such as breath control and emotion management are incredibly useful if you do not have them already. And you do not know how well you have developed them until you start working on them more. And finally, classes are a wonderful way to find people to work with.

Be comfortable changing up your routine a bit. In my own life, I found my biggest improvements came when I changed my routine out of necessity, or I decided to adopt better habits that added up over time. After all, you are what you do and think about day after day. Try taking a new action and set a plan before you are forced to because then it might be too late. This can all be accomplished by knowing what you want and not inadvertently contradicting your desire through the wrong actions.

For example, if you what you want is to make money as an actor, yet you keep finding reasons not to create content, or you keep applying only for unpaid jobs, then you could be inadvertently contradicting your desires. There are many great books written on this same principle and what some call "The Law of Attraction."

As you start to master your work (and we use the term master loosely here) you may uncover opportunities to teach. There is something called the 10,000-hour rule that suggests it takes 10,000 hours to master something. I imagine this is for the average person, and the average training. I believe people can learn much quicker given the proper methods of study.

I am not saying it does not take tremendous dedication and practice to develop mastery on certain things. It takes more time to master construction of a spaceship than it does a wooden table. What I am saying is that I believe we as people are much more capable of becoming proficient at concepts and physical feats than some would like to have you believe.

The more you learn, the more you can bring together to create a complete package of yourself. This may require you teaming up with others to balance out those activities you do not want to do or cannot manage to focus on for whatever reason. Hone in on your core skills as an actor and use the ideas on becoming a business from this book to grow.

Whenever you look for opportunities, remember that you are the product and service of your own business. As you succeed, more projects will find you, and you can help others succeed, and it just compounds. This industry requires new ways of thinking to stand out. By understanding some of the fundamental concepts of business, you can better prepare yourself. You can become greater than yourself.

In the end, remember to take some action that you find useful from this book. There are plenty of actionable ideas. Set a plan for yourself as it only takes a bit of time. Get something done today and go after what you want.

13. Ideas for Action

The complexities of creating a massive corporate entity are one thing. The foundational ideas in this book of doing business and working with others to bring products and services to the market is another. In this final chapter, I include a summary of the chapter and list ways you can apply the lessons in this book to your acting career and business by chapter.

Chapter 1. Entrepreneur

In Chapter 1. Entrepreneur, we examined how starting out as an actor, and building a long-term career as an actor is very much like entrepreneurship.

1) Look up how successful entrepreneurs and thought leaders view entrepreneurship via articles.

2) Make a list of your favorite entrepreneurs.

3) Look at something you accomplished recently and imagine what an entrepreneur might have done with it.

4) Research businesses started by your favorite celebrities.

5) Define entrepreneurship in your own words.

6) Explain why what you do is entrepreneurship.

7) List problems you can solve for others and how a business can be built around your solution.

8) Look up your favorite entrepreneurs and list their qualities.

9) Attend an entrepreneurship class.

10) Imagine a specific group of people you could appeal to.

Chapter 2. Framing Your Business

In Chapter 2. Framing Your Business, we examined many concepts you hear about when building a business and applied them to your business as an actor.

1) Pick a business idea from the chapter and relate it to your work.

2) List who you would like to be a business partner.

3) List who a coworker might be.

4) Imagine you were responsible for being your own agent and define how you would sell yourself.

5) Study a business outside of the industry and explain how their activities may be similar to yours.

6) Define what it means to build a team as an actor.

7) Watch a commercial with a celebrity in it and explain a few ways they could have made money from it.

8) Imagine how you might interact with a fan as if they were a customer while working as a salesperson.

9) List skills you developed from another workplace that can help you as an acting business.

10) Explain what products your favorite artists sold.

Chapter 3. Assessing Risk

In Chapter 3. Assessing Risk, we examined the concept of risk and how you can apply it to your business to create the highest chance of success.

1) Define risk in your own words.

2) Apply a percentage to your chance of success should you pursue a career as an actor.

3) Consider the risk if you continue to do what you are doing.

4) Do some research on the number of working actors around your country.

5) Consider back up plans.

6) Consider what you would do if you went all in.

7) Explain what it means to take a calculated risk.

8) Find ways you can "dabble" in your dream until you are more comfortable diving in, and explain how this reduces your risk.

9) Ask others about their experience becoming an actor.

10) Choose a movie you believe you could fit perfectly in.

Chapter 4. Deliver Value to Create Your Success

In Chapter 4. Deliver Value to Create Your Success we discussed the universal principle of giving enough value to deserve value back and how this is a fundamental principle of becoming successful.

1) List something you could sell for money right now, and explain why someone would buy it.

2) Explain something someone might value more than money.

3) List times when you provided a service for someone and got paid for it.

4) Explain why someone would pay to watch you perform.

5) List things you can provide that a director, producer, casting director, or audience might find valuable.

6) Look up an actor who is doing more with their business than just being an actor.

7) Explain how you can make someone feel valued.

8) Explain why art has value.

9) Explain how an actor can deliver value outside of just being skilled at their work.

10) Explain why a company might buy a product from one company over a similar product from another.

Chapter 5. Setting a Purpose

In Chapter 5. Setting a Purpose, we learned the guiding force of successful artists, business, and leader: a purpose.

1) Write down a purpose you could focus on trying to attain for at least the next five years.

2) Write down something you would like to achieve as an ultimate goal.

3) Find mission statements of companies you admire.

4) List other times you wrote down goals and achieved them.

5) Find people you admire and imagine what kind of goals they set for themselves.

6) List specific easy actions you can take towards your goal.

7) Celebrate a recent win you had.

8) Take a goal you currently have and make it bigger.

9) Create a simple plan that can help you accomplish one of your current goals.

10) Take your favorite company, research their number of employees, and consider the force if all their employees worked towards the same goal.

Chapter 6. Creativity

In Chapter 6. Creativity, we looked at the forces that drive the entertainment industry and ideas for how you can contribute.

1) Write down a daydream you have and how it can be turned into a movie.

2) Explain how the film industry brings both creative and technical people together to accomplish the same goal.

3) Name people who you feel comfortable sharing ideas with.

4) Pick a goal and list a few different creative ways you can accomplish the same purpose.

5) Explain how creativity can solve business problems.

6) Explain why creativity requires confidence to bloom.

7) Consider an idea from a top entrepreneur or your favorite movie and think about why someone else bought into their idea.

8) Find a product you use all the time and research the history of it.

9) Study the life of an inventor and apply that to your life.

10) Explain how your creativity is unique to you.

Chapter 7. Business Model

In Chapter 7. Business Model, we define what a business model is and explained ways you can come up with unique ways to improve the way you work.

1) Find an advertisement for something free online and explain how someone can make money from it.

2) Pick a restaurant you like and examine what they do differently from the others.

3) List a few ways you can make money as an actor outside of just getting paid directly from a movie.

4) Define the relationship between a production company that pays you and a fan that pays you.

5) List some products you would be comfortable representing.

6) Take something you did successfully in your business as an actor, and examine how you can repeat that success.

7) Learn about franchises and their business models.

8) Read up on the concept of upselling and cross-selling.

9) Tie in the concepts from chapter 4 on delivering value with this chapter on business models.

10) Consider how you can create a profitable business model providing free content on a free video distribution platform.

Chapter 8. Money Management

In Chapter 8. Money Management, we evaluated the financial differences in being an actor versus creating a regular business, and how you can overcome those differences.

1) Explain why a bank may be more likely to loan money to a restaurant owner with a business plan than an actor with a business plan.

2) Pick a list of products or services you spend a lot of money on and pick one to eliminate.

3) Write out the exact amount of money you want in the future, and how you will spend it.

4) Read a book that might help provide information to fix a financial challenge you are having.

5) Make a list of expenses that were truly used for your business and separate them from anything unrelated to your business.

6) Research residual income.

7) Define what your proof of concept as an actor looks like, and even though a bank might not finance you, find someone who may help in other ways.

8) Make a list of executive producers on your favorite shows.

9) Examine why a bank will invest money in a major studio but not a smaller production.

10) Set a date to speak with an accountant or financial advisor at your bank.

Chapter 9. Your Team

In Chapter 9. Your Team, we look what it means to build a team as an actor by reframing the traditional business concept.

1) List a series of teams you have been a part of and how you contributed to them.

2) Explain the importance of how a team can multiply its' efforts by working towards the same goal.

3) Explain what you might look for in a professional business partner.

4) List a few notable dynamic duos.

5) Imagine what your ideal team would look like.

6) Explain how someone who does not know you can be a part of your team, or you theirs.

7) Pick someone you admire and plan a way to contact them.

8) Explain how building a team can contribute to greater prosperity for all.

9) Find someone you can mentor.

10) Find and read five articles that discuss networking and the importance of relationships.

Chapter 10. Growing Your Business

In Chapter 10. Growing Your Business, we went over concepts such as sales and marketing and applied them to building an acting career.

1) List some opportunities created by new social media platforms and production technology.

2) Research some sales and marketing concepts such as sales funnels, cold-calling, and presentation skills.

3) Differentiate between the different departments of your acting career that we discussed in Chapter 10.

4) Explain how an actor who is a household might delegate their work.

5) List a challenge you might have as your career takes off and write a way to overcome that challenge.

6) Explain how an actor who started their career 20 years ago might have to do business differently today.

7) Define what it means to protect your business and likeness.

8) Explain a cyclical trend an actor might experience with regards to their success and popularity.

9) Research what it takes to create a business entity, and explain when it might be necessary to do so.

10) Look up some successful producers, actors, and directors and their companies.

Chapter 11. Being Loved

In Chapter 11. Being Loved, we discuss the importance of being an actor that people will love and respect because businesses succeed when they have products or services that people love.

1) Explain how giving value can result in being loved.

2) Explain how you can be loveable while being a tough, respected leader.

3) List three ways you can show love to others.

4) Explain the importance of being tolerant of others.

5) List the costs of being despised.

6) Define the skills you have when dealing with people.

7) Explain how a controversial artist can still be loved.

8) List people who have shown you love recently.

9) Explain why it might be easier to be loved than feared and vice versa.

10) Research how a household brand might show love to large groups of fans.

Chapter 12. Keep Learning

In Chapter 12. Keep Learning, we discuss how successful people are constantly learning, and how you can do this affordably.

1) Name something you learned recently.

2) Read a biography about someone you admire.

3) Consider something you can do differently and learn about the method you plan to use.

4) Find some useful publications to subscribe to.

5) Find a nearby library to visit and stay there and read up on anything you want to learn.

6) Explain how you can apply a skill you learned in the past to something you are doing now.

7) Write about something you are learning or have learned about.

8) Plan a book that can teach what you know to others.

9) Explain a few ways the concepts in this book have helped you redefine your career.

10) Create some action tasks right now and prosper!

With any business, there is no guarantee of success. Even formulas created by great franchises have risks associated or huge start-up challenges such as acquiring financial backing. It is up to you to adapt the principles you find the most relevant to yourself and persevere as you start to face greater challenges. And by doing so, chances are you will find what it is you want.

About the Editor

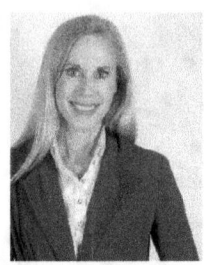 Kathleen Roy has a BFA in Theatre, an MA in Theatre, an MFA in Acting for Television and Film as well as a certification in secondary education. Since she has spent many years in classrooms both as a student and college professor, she has had to edit many pieces of writing. She is also a writer of screenplays and recently published a book of original monologues for actors entitled "Monologues for the 21st Century Woman".

Kathleen taught communications, public speaking and theatre for most of her life until moving to Los Angeles to become a professional film actor. She continues to teach what she is most passionate about, which is theatre, in an online course. She still enjoys acting on the stage but has delved into the world of filmmaking both in front of the camera and behind it. She creates content and produces original short films. She recommends this book as a great tool to help the actor succeed!

About the Author

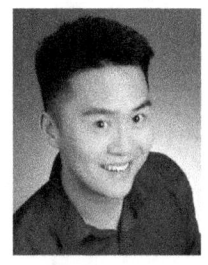

Emmett Ferguson has an MBA from the Jack Welch Management Institute and wrote this book out of a desire to combine his interests in business and the film industry. He is a member of SAG-AFTRA and is also the author of "Like Your Way to Success: How to Use Social Media to Get What You Want" and "Don't Be Selfish, Share Your Art with the World" which urges artists to pursue their creative endeavors.

Over a period of many years, Emmett made his way to the Greater Los Angeles Area. During this time, he focused a significant amount of time and effort to combine the thoughts and ideas from many different experiences to create this book.

Your first step might make you highly successful, or maybe your first ten thousand steps might not work, but no matter what, nothing happens' without doing.